941.608 Hewitt, James.
HEW
    The Irish question.

BRANCH

$18.60

DATE			

Cover *A typical scene in war-torn Belfast.*

Frontispiece *The funeral of two IRA men, shot by an undercover soldier, is watched by a young boy in Londonderry, May 1981.*

THE
IRISH
QUESTION

James Hewitt

ROURKE ENTERPRISES, INC.
Vero Beach, Florida 32964

FLASHPOINTS

First published in the United States in 1987 by
Rourke Enterprises Inc PO Box 3328 Vero Beach Florida
32964

First published in 1986 by Wayland (Publishers) Ltd
61 Western Road, Hove East Sussex BN3 1JD, England

© Copyright 1986 Wayland (Publishers) Ltd

Manufactured by The Bath Press, Avon, England

Library of Congress Cataloging-in-Publication Data
Hewitt, James
   The Irish question.
   (Flashpoints)
   Bibliography: p.
   Includes index.
   Summary: Examines the conflict in Ireland
between the Irish and the English, with an emphasis
on events occurring since 1969, and discusses
treaties and other possible solutions.
   1. Northern Ireland—Politics and government—
1969–   —Juvenile literature.   2. Irish question—
Juvenile literature.   [1. Northern Ireland—
Politics and government—1969–   .   2. Irish
question]   I. Title   II. Series: Flashpoints
DA990U46H46   1986   941.60824   86–20274
ISBN 0-86592-027-3

Contents

1
Two tribes

The Protestant Apprentice Boys' March, Londonderry, August 1985.

On Tuesday, August 12, 1969, Protestant Apprentice Boys held their annual march in Londonderry, commemorating the shutting of the city gates at the approach of the Catholic army of James II in 1688. Because of clashes earlier in 1969 and in the preceding autumn, between Catholic civil rights supporters, police, and militant Protestants, the atmosphere in the city was tense. Rioting broke out, and lasted two days. In the Catholic Bogside district, women and children made bombs from bottles filled with gasoline. Along with broken paving stones these were hurled by youths and men at the police, who replied with tear gas. More than one hundred people were injured, ninety of them policemen.

Worse was to come. In Belfast, Catholics and Protestants had already rioted on the 4th, setting shops on fire. On the night of the 14th, violence again erupted in working-class West Belfast, in an area where Catholic and Protestant districts rubbed shoulders. Catholic youths flaunted a banned Irish Republican flag and sang the national anthem of the Republic. Enraged Protestants attacked them. Soon entire streets of houses were ablaze. Many Catholics fled their

Riots in Belfast, August 4, 1969.

homes to spend the night in schools and community centers in safer areas; some kept going until they crossed the border into the Irish Republic. In Belfast, shots were exchanged between the rival factions. The police took to the riot-torn streets in armored cars and in some places opened fire with machine guns. In two days of rioting in the capital, 10 people were killed, 145 were injured, and 200 houses were destroyed by fire.

The civil violence that broke out in August 1969 in both Londonderry (or Derry, the original name which the Catholics prefer to use) and Belfast ended in an important way—with the deployment of British troops. The prime minister of Northern Ireland, Major James Chichester Clark, had requested military aid, which was granted by the British home secretary, James Callaghan, after urgent consultations with Prime Minister Harold Wilson. British soldiers

A hooded youth uses a slingshot to hurl stones at British soldiers in Belfast, following the death of IRA hunger striker, Bobby Sands, in the Maze prison, May 5, 1981.

11

took up positions in both cities in flashpoint areas, first in Londonderry and then in Belfast.

James Callaghan told Gerry Fitt (later Lord Fitt), the Member of Parliament (MP) at Westminster for West Belfast:"It's one thing to send them in. It's another thing to get them out." They were prophetic words. Since 1969, the British Army and the Royal Ulster Constabulary (Northern Ireland's police force) have been subjected to frequent

Flagwaving for the Northern Ireland prime minister, Major James Chichester Clark, in a Protestant area of Belfast, 1969.

attacks from the Irish Republican Army (IRA), and terrorist bombings have killed or maimed many civilians. Protestant reprisals have also taken the form of sectarian killings.

An all too familiar scene in Belfast, 1969.

Over a period of sixteen years (1969–85), nearly 2,500 people have died in the longest sustained period of civil violence in European history. The proportional figure for community warfare in mainland Britain would be nearly 100,000 violent deaths!

13

Evidence of a divided community: **above**, *the ancient order of Hibernians, a Catholic group, parade in Country Antrim ...*

In 1969, the problem of the Irish Question became more acute for the British government. During nearly fifty years of Unionist rule by Protestants in Northern Ireland, successive British governments had been able to avert their gaze from the grievances of the Catholic minority there. The escalation of violence changed that, and reawakened Protestant insecurity. Now, from television, radio, and newspapers, millions of people in Britain and abroad were learning of a divided society in Northern Ireland, of two conflicting communities or "tribes"—Protestant and Catholic, Unionist and Nationalist, Loyalist and Republican, Orange and Green. One is determined to stay British and keep the northeastern part of the island independent of the Republic; the other is clinging to an Irish identity and wanting to belong to a free republic throughout Ireland. Communities with separate political and religious allegiances; separate national identities; separate anniversaries, banners, bands, and marching tunes; separate districts, villages, housing developments; separate pubs and social clubs; separate secret societies; separate doctors, dentists, attorneys. Even a person's name can signify from which community he or she comes.

In 1972, the British government suspended the Northern Ireland Parliament and began direct rule of a strife-torn province. There has been a state of crisis ever since, with sporadic bouts of violence by Catholics and Protestants.

. . . and **below,** *the annual 12th of July Parade, in which the Protestants celebrate William of Orange's victory at the Battle of the Boyne.*

On partition of Ireland in 1921, six of the nine counties of the ancient province of Ulster became Northern Ireland.

Opposite *A young boy, symbol of the fighting in Northern Ireland; wearing an oversized gas mask, gasoline bomb in hand and a map of the problem on his jacket.*

Boundary of Northern Ireland
---- Boundary of the Province of Ulster

SCOTLAND

Donegal
Londonderry
London-derry
Antrim
Tyrone
ULSTER
Belfast
Fermanagh
Down
Armagh
Monaghan
Cavan

CONNACHT

Dublin

LEINSTER

MUNSTER

All attempts to find a political consensus between them have so far failed. It is one of the world's most intractable problems, a political impasse that has come about as a result both of Ireland's complex past and troubled modern history.

Ireland as a whole is comprised of thirty-two counties: twenty-six in the Republic, and the remaining six (Tyrone, Armagh, Londonderry, Down, Antrim and Fermanagh) forming Northern Ireland. The ancient province of Ulster consisted of these six counties plus three others, now belonging to the Republic. The division of Ireland in this way after World War I has caused as many problems as it was originally meant to solve. In Northern Ireland, Protestants are in an approximate three-to-two majority, while in the island overall there are more Catholics than Protestants. Hence each group in Northern Ireland feels constantly threatened by the other, and this fear and hostility breeds violence. Why has this arisen, and is there any way out of the conflict?

2
A troubled history

"Then came the Great War. Every institution almost in the world was strained, great empires had been overturned, the whole map of Europe has been changed ... But as the deluge subsides, and as the waters fall short, we see the dreary steeples of Fermanagh and Tyrone emerging once again. The integrity of their quarrel is one of the few institutions that has been unaltered in the cataclysm that has swept the world."

Winston Churchill made that speech in 1922. The "quarrel" goes back more than three hundred years, but the roots of the Irish problem may be said to go back a further five centuries when Henry II sent over to Ireland a group of Anglo-Norman nobles, led by Strongbow. From then on, the story of Ireland is one of increasing English control and strong Irish resistance.

English kings were content with the title "Lord of Ireland" until, in 1541, Henry VIII had himself, and his successors, declared "King of Ireland." Seven years earlier he had made the Church in England independent of the pope in Rome. From then on the bulk of the Irish population, whose allegiance remained with Rome, would feel alienated both from English rule and the English Church.

The flight of the Earls

Elizabeth I had to overcome a series of uprisings by Irish Gaelic chiefs. The most serious opposition came from Hugh O'Neill of Ulster, who was finally subdued in March 1603. O'Neill, Earl of Tyrone, and O'Donnell, Earl of Tryconnel, and ninety-eight other Irish chiefs went into exile on the European mainland. English and Scottish Lowland settlers, mainly of Protestant and Presbyterian denominations, took possession of the vacant land. Many native Irish were employed by settlers, and some farmed land and paid rents to absentee landlords.

Opposite *Henry VIII, who alienated the Irish by breaking away from the Catholic Church and declaring himself head of the Church of England.*

18

Oliver Cromwell, who took his New Model Army to Ireland to put down the rebellion.

Rebellion and plantation

In 1641, a great rebellion against the settlers began in Ulster, and several thousand English and Scottish immigrants were murdered. In the wake of their success the rebels set up a government at Kilkenny in 1642. Oliver Cromwell, however, was determined to restore puritan, Protestant supremacy. So in August 1649, he took the New Model Army to Ireland and spent nine months there putting down the rebellion with a severity not forgotten by Irish Catholics. Cromwell confiscated large areas of land and gave it to settlers and some of his soldiers. By 1665, Protestants made up one-third of the population of Ireland, but owned four-fifths of the land.

Cromwell's severity and his "plantation" policy of establishing Protestants as landowners in Ireland united the Catholics in opposition. They naturally sided with James II, a Catholic, in his struggle with William of Orange for the throne of England. After reigning for just three years

(1665–68), James fled to France and William, Prince of Orange, a Protestant, was invited to succeed him. To gain support for his claim to the English throne, James landed in Ireland on March 12, 1689, where a Catholic army awaited him. Thousands of Ulster Protestants fled to England; others were besieged in Enniskillen and Londonderry. As James had the support of French officers and troops, provided by Louis XIV, the Catholics were powerful enough to organize an Irish Parliament, which then passed an Act returning to Catholics the land seized by Cromwell.

The Battle of the Boyne

It never came into force, however, because William defeated James in 1690 at the Battle of the Boyne, annually celebrated by Protestant Orangemen on July 12. When Catholic gentry fled with James's soldiers to the European mainland, their vacant lands were given to Protestant settlers. The present distribution of Catholics and Protestants in Ulster can thus be traced back to the seventeenth-century plantations. A large number of Catholics remained, but most of them lived on the poorest land. William was not himself a bigot, but his victory marked the beginning of secure Protestant power in Ireland—and of two fixed communities in Ulster with separate allegiances and identities.

Orangemen unfurl the banner of William III.

3
A tradition of violence

Irish terrorist bombing of London underground trains and stations; the headquarters of the Special Branch at Scotland Yard blown up; a bomb blast and fire at the Tower of London; and on the same day explosions in Westminster Hall and in the chamber of the House of Commons, most damage occurring where the prime minister sits... These dramatic events were as devastating as the Harrods or Brighton bombings of recent memory. But they may sound less familiar because they happened one hundred years ago, between 1883 and 1885.

United Irishmen
Republican revolutionary violence goes back a long way. Its first heroes were Theobald Wolfe Tone, a Presbyterian, and other leaders of the United Irishmen, a secret society inspired by ideas of liberty and brotherhood observed in the French Revolution of 1789. Originating among Ulster Presbyterians, the movement worked for Catholic and Presbyterian emancipation from British and Protestant subjection. Their failed rebellion of 1798 was Catholic in the south and mainly Presbyterian in the north. Like the Catholics, Presbyterians (whose faith is a nonconformist form of Protestantism) did not have full civil rights, and this bound the two groups together. However, Catholics and Presbyterians in Ulster were not to find common cause again.

One outcome of the rebellion was the Act of Union of 1800, whereby a partly independent Irish Parliament was abolished, and Ireland became part of the United Kingdom of Great Britain and Ireland. The northern Presbyterians were given full rights and settled down within the fabric of a Protestant ascendancy in Ireland that alienated Catholics, some of whom continued to join secret societies bent on ending English rule by force.

The men who waged a "dynamite war" against British cities a century ago were Fenians—members of the Irish

Opposite *The wreckage at the Grand Hotel, Brighton, England, after the IRA bomb attack during the Conservative Party Conference, 1984.*

Charles Stewart Parnell MP, the Irish Nationalist, who led the Irish Home Rule movement at Westminster.

Republican Brotherhood. Many American settlers had originally sailed from Ireland and now gave support to this secret revolutionary organization. Today Irish ballads recall the tradition of "the bold Fenian men," whose aim was to force the British out of Ireland. Yet the Fenians represented a small minority of the Irish people. In the late nineteenth century, the main weight of Irish nationalist feeling centered on the constitutional campaign for Home Rule—for an Irish Parliament as there had been before the Act of Union.

Home Rule or "Rome Rule"?

In 1893, Gladstone's Second Home Rule Bill was defeated in the House of Lords, but in 1912 Asquith's New Home Rule Bill was passed in the House of Commons and by then the House of Lords could delay a Bill for only two years. This meant that the Bill would become law in 1914. The Ulster Unionists – Protestants loyal to the union with Great Britain – were alarmed. To them, Home Rule meant both loss of their British identity and "Rome Rule"

A Victorian cartoon, depicting the agitation for the repeal of the Union.

Protestant slogans on a wall in the York Road area of Belfast.

(domination by the Roman Catholic Church) – fears still strong today. They organized mass demonstrations against Home Rule and 471,000 of them signed "a solemn league and covenant" (some using their own blood for ink) vowing to use "all means which may be necessary to defeat the present conspiracy to set up a Home Rule parliament in Ireland." They showed they meant it. One-hundred thousand Unionists joined the Ulster Volunteer Force (UVF, now an illegal paramilitary organization), and drilled with arms shipped in from Germany. The southern Nationalists, not to be outdone, formed their own Irish Volunteer Force, and also brought in weapons from Germany.

The Easter Rising

With Ireland at explosion point, World War I (1914–18) began. The Ulster Volunteer Force became the 36th (Ulster) Division who fought so bravely for Britain at the Battle of the Somme, suffering appalling casualties. In the south, the Irish Volunteers were split into those who supported the Allies' involvement in the war and those who—as hard-line Republicans—saw "England's extremity as Ireland's opportunity" for insurrection. On Easter Sunday, 1916, rebels seized the center of Dublin, declared a Republic, and

O'Connell Street, Dublin, after the Easter Rising in 1916.

27

Eamon de Valera, president of Sinn Fein, inspecting the illegal Irish Republican Army in 1923.

held out for a week. Fourteen rebel leaders were subsequently executed, evoking a wave of public sympathy for the Irish cause. Support for independence now grew fast. In the general election of 1918, the Republican party, Sinn Fein, won seventy-three seats. They shunned Westminster and set up the first "Dail" or Irish Parliament. The most militant Republicans organized themselves as an illegal paramilitary movement, the Irish Republican Army (IRA), and launched attacks on British security forces.

Partition

The Government of Ireland Act of December 1920 brought in partition, and an Anglo-Irish Treaty was signed in 1921. Twenty-six of the thirty-two counties of Ireland became the Irish Free State, with dominion status, and the remaining six counties became part of the United Kingdom of Great Britain and Northern Ireland. The Unionists accepted partition reluctantly. Hardline Republicans in the south saw anything less than all-Ireland independence as a "sellout," and a bitter civil war was fought in 1922 between pro-Treaty and anti-Treaty forces, in which more than 600 people were killed and over 3,000 wounded. The pro-Treaty faction won. The main political parties of the Irish Republic, Fine Gael and Fianna Fail, stem from those bitter days of fighting, representing the pro-Treaty and the anti-Treaty sides respectively.

The present day provisional IRA, at a press conference.

Sinn Fein continued as the political wing of the IRA. A smaller, more extreme organization, the Irish National Liberation Army (INLA), which has links with left-wing revolutionary groups abroad, has since been formed, and the IRA has now split into two factions. The Official IRA are against the use of violence, while the Provisional IRA (or "Provos") are prepared to use any means to attack what they see as British occupation of Ireland in the "six counties." There, in 1922, the Protestant Unionists had a two-thirds majority and were settling down to the start of what would be more than fifty years of unbroken rule.

Party members discuss Unionist Party political posters at their headquarters in Belfast.

4
Unbroken Unionist rule

Although the Ulster Unionists settled reluctantly for the partitioning of Ireland, with about one million Protestants in the six counties of Northern Ireland compared to half a million Catholics, they were able to take power and hold it for fifty years without a break. During that half century, election after election for the Ulster Parliament at Stormont or at Westminster was fought on one overriding issue for the voter: Are you for or against Northern Ireland staying within the United Kingdom? Beside the issue of Northern Ireland's very existence, social issues paled into insignificance and were neglected. From the start, voting patterns followed Unionist/Protestant versus Nationalist/Catholic lines that are still in force.

Posters near a Catholic polling station urge voters not to support the listed parties.

Relatives visit prisoners arrested during the Easter Uprising in Dublin, 1916.

Siege and rebellion

The Unionist community is often said to have a "siege mentality" that can be traced back to seventeenth-century plantation days. From the start, the Royal Ulster Constabulary (RUC), had to cope with unusual strain for a police force. Hence they were armed against attacks from the IRA and to control the sectarian fighting that had taken 400 lives by the summer of 1922. Most Catholics opposed the existence of Northern Ireland, and few were prepared to cooperate in running its institutions. It was some years before Nationalists agreed to take their seats in the Stormont Parliament. In such an atmosphere, it was easy for many Protestants to view every Catholic as a "Fenian" or rebel.

Catholics, on the other hand, found themselves in what Northern Ireland's first prime minister, Lord Craigavon, described as "A Protestant nation and a Protestant state," while Irish people in the south had a Free State and an

1922: an armored car used by Free State troops in the civil war that broke out after the signing of the Anglo-Irish Treaty in 1921.

The last of the British Army leaving the Irish Free State in 1922.

Irish Gaelic identity. It was this same Gaelic and Catholic identity that Unionists wanted no part of. They felt their worst fears were confirmed when the Free State's Irish Constitution of 1937 included articles acknowledging the special position of the Roman Catholic Church and claiming that "The national territory consists of the whole island of Ireland, its islands and territorial seas."

During World War II the Free State maintained neutrality. Northern Ireland's contribution to victory was praised by Winston Churchill, who had seriously considered seizing some Irish ports during the war.

It was not until 1948 that the Irish Free State left the British Commonwealth and became a Republic. The British (Labour) government responded with the Ireland Act of 1949, which guaranteed that the status of Northern Ireland as part of the United Kingdom would not be changed without the consent of the Parliament of Northern Ireland.

The civil rights movement

During the 1960s there were many civil rights marches and demonstrations in the United States and throughout Europe. A civil rights movement was started in Northern Ireland in 1967, demanding an end to discrimination against Catholics in employment, in housing allocation, and in local government franchise.

The Irish Citizen Army parade at Liberty Hall, Dublin, 1915. The banner declares an attitude that was mirrored by the Irish Free State during World War II.

Protestants were the major employers in industry and trade, and tended to promote Protestant workers. In the public sector it was alleged that Unionist-controlled councils mainly employed Protestants; therefore, few Catholics got the better jobs. Sir Basil Brooke, prime minister of Northern Ireland from 1944–63, had made a speech as minister for agriculture in 1934 in which he said, "I recommend those people who are Loyalist not to employ Roman Catholics, ninety-five percent of whom are disloyal."

To compound the problem, many Catholics chose not to work in Loyalist areas, and Protestant businessmen likewise refused to locate industry in staunchly Republican areas. To complete the segregation, Catholic employers preferred to employ Catholic workers. As one Unionist politician put it: "There is no discrimination against Catholics; anyway, the other side does it, too." Undoubtedly, Catholics suffered the more severe discrimination, because the weight of financial power lay with the Protestants.

Sir Basil Brooke, prime minister of Northern Ireland from 1944–63, with Lady Brooke.

Unionist discrimination

Civil rights campaigners were also able to point to discrimination against Catholics in council housing allocation. It was alleged, too, that the siting of housing developments was used to support "gerrymandering"—the fixing of constituency boundaries so that Catholics were isolated in small groups and hence Protestant voters were more likely to gain their choice of MP. For example, in the County Borough of Londonderry, although sixty percent of the adult population was Catholic, Unionists held sixty percent of the seats. The Unionists were also helped by a franchise system – which lasted in Northern Ireland until 1969 although in England it had been discontinued by the Attlee government after World War II – whereby householders and spouses had a vote but not adult children. This placed at a disadvantage families where several generations shared a house—an extended family pattern more traditional among Catholics.

Belfast members of the "B Specials" parade through the streets on their way to a church service, 1970.

Bernadette Devlin, addressing a civil rights rally in London, 1969.

The civil rights campaign began at a time when the Ulster prime minister, Captain Terence O'Neill, was encouraging Catholics to feel more a part of Northern Irish society. He visited a Catholic school and hospital, and exchanged visits with Sean Lemass, the Republic's prime minister. However the more militant Unionists, such as the Reverend Ian Paisley, saw the civil rights movement as a Republican plot against the state. Inevitably there were those who wished to use it as such. MP Bernadette Devlin, one of the leaders of the movement, admitted in August 1979: "The whole national question was reopened. It stopped being about civil rights the day it started on the streets. The leaders lost control by October 1968.'' In that month, a banned civil rights march proceeded in Londonderry and the police used batons against the marchers. Then, in January 1969, students at Queen's University, Belfast, staged a three-day march for civil rights from Belfast to Londonderry. As they reached Burntollet Bridge, near Londonderry, on January 4, the marchers were attacked by Protestants armed with nail-studded sticks. The clashes were witnessed worldwide on television screens.

A civil rights march in Lurgan in April 1979.

British troops deployed

It was with tension still high in the cities of Londonderry and Belfast that very serious rioting broke out in August 1969, leading to the deployment of British troops on the streets. At first the British soldiers were welcomed by the Catholics as protectors, but the harmony did not last long. The troops soon had to put down rioting in Catholic areas. In Belfast, tear gas was used for the first time in Britain to control civil disturbances.

Bloody Sunday and Direct Rule

During the 1970s, two further developments aroused strong anti-British feeling in many Catholics. The first was the increased use of internment without trial during 1971. It had always been possible under the Civil Authorities (Special Powers) Act (NI) 1922, and had been used before to

The British Army maintain a constant presence in Belfast, but everyday life still continues.

40

counter IRA campaigns, but suddenly its use was more widespread. Protestant extremists were arrested and held too, but by far the greatest number of loud knocks on doors in the early morning were at the homes of Catholics. The second thing that disastrously worsened Catholic-British relationships were the events of "Bloody Sunday." On January 30, 1972, civil rights marchers (possibly infiltrated by members of the IRA) defied a ban and moved forward in Londonderry. Police and paratroopers decided to restrict the march to Nationalist areas. The Army were subjected to an attack of some sort, which they claim came from small-arms fire, whereupon they opened fire themselves. Thirteen Catholic demonstrators were shot dead, yet the victims appeared to be unarmed.

A search for escaped Republican detainees in Belfast, 1972.

An injured British soldier is helped by his comrade.

The IRA responded by mounting a campaign of bombing in which many innocent civilians died or were horribly maimed. Military and police patrols were also attacked. Between 1969 and 1979 more than 300 British soldiers were killed in Northern Ireland, along with more than 200 members of the police and reserve forces. By March 1972, the British government felt that the problem of security in Northern Ireland was so serious that Westminster would have to take control of the running of the province. On March 24, the Stormont Parliament was suspended and Direct Rule introduced.

A soldier stands guard at the Parliament Building, Stormont, home of the government of Northern Ireland in Belfast.

5
Poles apart

The ending of the Stormont Parliament and the imposition of Direct Rule in 1972 angered Loyalists. Their paramilitary Ulster Defence Association organized the erection of barricades in Protestant areas, using hijacked trucks and buses. Hooded men paraded, carrying clubs. For some months previously, Catholics had barricaded *their* areas in Londonderry and Belfast. In an attempt to defuse ghetto warfare the British Army eventually broke up both the Loyalist and Nationalist barricades.

The Belfast battalion of the paramilitary UDA, at the start of their parade, 1972.

British Army troops help Catholic residents to pull down a barricade in the Falls Road area of Belfast.

A border referendum was held in March 1973. Fifty-eight percent of the voting population voted for maintaining Northern Ireland's union with Great Britain. One percent voted for a united Ireland. Forty-one percent failed to vote. Nationalist politicians had called for a poll boycott, on the grounds that only a vote by all the Irish people was relevant, not just those in six counties. Allowing for habitual non-voters (twenty to twenty-five percent), the poll figures showed that Protestants had voted solidly for the union and that most Catholics had abstained from voting.

Safeguard for Loyalists

The border poll was followed by the Northern Ireland Constitution Act, which guaranteed Northern Ireland's Loyalists that they would not cease to stay part of the United Kingdom "without the consent of the majority of the people of Northern Ireland voting in a poll." This amended a guarantee of the Ireland Act of 1949, which had said "without the consent of the Parliament of Northern Ireland."

Elections were held for a Northern Ireland Assembly, with predictable results: sixty-two Unionists and twenty-five Nationalists were elected, with the proportional representation system allowing the cross-communal Alliance Party to pick up nine seats. The Northern Ireland secretary, William Whitelaw, persuaded leaders of the Unionists, the Social Democratic and Labour Party (the SDLP, the main nationalist party), and the Alliance Party to form a power-sharing Executive. The SDLP agreed, on condition that an "Irish dimension" be introduced. By that they meant giving the Republic's government an interest.

Loyalists marching to Stormont in 1971, in support of William Craig for prime minister.

The Rev. Ian Paisley, addressing a rally in Oxford against the pope's visit to Britain in 1982.

Attempts at consensus

To that end, an Anglo-Irish summit conference was held at Sunningdale in late 1973. It was agreed that a Council of Ireland would be set up, which representatives from the Republic and Northern Ireland would attend. Such a Council had been planned in 1920, but did not materialize. Nor did it this time. The power-sharing Executive functioned for a few months, under the leadership of a former Northern Ireland prime minister, Brian Faulkner, but was brought down in May by a Protestant Loyalist workers' strike. The Assembly was dissolved. Since then all attempts have failed to find a political consensus in Northern Ireland that would enable the British government to transfer or devolve power to the province.

A soldier hides next to a poster of the hunger strikers who died in the Maze prison.

Extremism grows

Meanwhile, the Reverend Ian Paisley's Democratic Unionists had won eleven seats in the 1973 Assembly elections and was gaining influence. There was also growing support for the Republican party, Sinn Fein, which was fueled by the deaths during hunger strike of ten IRA prisoners. They used this traditional Republican tactic to protest against being treated as criminal rather than political prisoners. The hunger strikes were preceded by a period of wearing blankets instead of uniforms and of smearing cells with excrement—the "blanket" and "dirty" protests.

In 1980, an alternative approach was sought. The prime ministers of Britain and Ireland, Margaret Thatcher and Charles Haughey, met and agreed to set up an Anglo-Irish Intergovernmental Council. This allowed for meetings between ministers and civil servants from both countries.

British Prime Minister Margaret Thatcher chatting to crowds over a security fence in Belfast, 1981.

6
The New Ireland Forum

Youngsters give the "thumbs up" sign beneath the walls of a house covered with IRA prisoners' demands.

The first session of the New Ireland Forum was held in Dublin Castle on May 30, 1983, and its report was issued a year later. It "was established for consultations on the manner in which lasting peace and stability could be achieved in a 'New Ireland' through the democratic process and to report on the possible new structures and processes through which this objective might be achieved." It was participated in by leaders and members of the three main political parties in the Republic – Fianna Fail, Fine Gael, and the Labour Party – and by the main Nationalist party

from the north, the Social Democratic and Labour Party. The Unionists boycotted the Forum, but unionist opinion was obtained through some written submissions and oral presentations.

The report set out "the major realities" of the Northern Ireland problem, which included "the failure to recognize and accommodate the identity of northern Nationalists, resulting in their alienation from the system of political authority." At the same time, it acknowledged the need for Nationalists to recognize and accommodate in a New Ireland the British and Protestant identity and ethos of the Unionists.

Rejecting the use of violence, the Forum Report said that a settlement should be negotiated based on acceptance of the validity of both Nationalist and Unionist identities, with no tradition allowed to dominate the other.

Canvassing on behalf of Paddy Agnew, a prisoner in the Maze prison, who contested the Irish general election in Co. Louth.

The case for a United Ireland

Three solutions to the Northern Ireland problem were discussed in detail: a unitary state (a united Ireland), a federal or confederal state, and joint authority. It was decided that "the best and most durable basis for peace and stability" would be "a united Ireland in the form of a sovereign, independent Irish state to be achieved peacefully and by consent." In a united Ireland, Unionist and Nationalist identities would be protected and preserved. Unionists could hold joint British and Irish citizenship. "The state could develop structures, relationships, and associations with Britain which could include an Irish–British Council with intergovernmental and interparliamentary structures which would acknowledge the unique relationship between Ireland and Britain and which would express the long-established connection which Unionists have with Britain."

The confederal alternative

Also discussed was a two state federal or confederal Ireland based on the existing southern and northern identities, each of which would have a measure of autonomy, with its own parliament and executive. "In a federation, residual power

A massive police presence at a march in Dublin in 1981, in support of the dead hunger strikers.

A young man makes his opinions clear on a Belfast wall.

would rest with the central government. Certain powers would be vested in the two individual states. A confederation would comprise the two states which would delegate certain specified powers to a confederal government... In a confederal arrangement, the powers held at the center could be relatively limited (for example, foreign policy, external and internal security policy, and perhaps, currency and monetary policy) ..." Although Protestants are in a minority in Ireland as a whole, a federal or confederal arrangement would give Unionists some power and influence in a new Ireland.

The third solution discussed in detail was joint authority, with the London and Dublin governments having equal responsibility for running Northern Ireland. Under joint authority the Unionist and Nationalist communities in Northern Ireland would find equality.

The British all-party Kilbrandon Committee considered the Forum Report and solutions to the Ulster crisis. The majority of members supported what they called "cooperative devolution." They recommended setting up a ministerial executive that would have one British minister, one Irish minister, as well as three elected representatives from Northern Ireland.

7
Possible solutions?

There may appear to be a wide choice of potential solutions to Northern Ireland's problems, but so far each one has run up against insurmountable opposition. For most Irish Nationalists there is only one solution to the Ulster crisis—unification. It is the centuries-old aspiration for which much blood has been spilled. Some Nationalists would settle for federation/confederation or some form of joint authority, though perhaps only as a stage on the way to a unitary state.

The British political parties do not oppose unification, providing the majority of people in Northern Ireland support it. They don't. To the Protestant Unionist majority, the very idea is unthinkable. They fear losing their British and Protestant heritage. They point to a different, Gaelic culture in the south and to the powerful influence of the Roman Catholic Church: for example, legislation inspired by Church teachings against birth control, divorce, and abortion.

Loyal Ulster Protestants beneath banners proclaiming their beliefs, 1947.

A woman's face alight with joy as she joins in prayers for peace at an interdenominational peace service at Downpatrick Cathedral, 1981.

The shape of a "New Ireland"

As we saw in the New Ireland Forum Report, Republican politicians are now, belatedly, aware of the need to placate Unionist fears, and to point out that a unified Ireland would be pluralistic—a Catholic/Protestant Ireland in which the identity of the northern Protestants would be recognized and accommodated. Some people in the Republic fear that the influence of one million northern Protestants in a united Ireland of nearly five million people, might undermine traditional Catholic values. On the other hand, there are many Irish people in the Republic who find invigorating the thought of a "New Ireland." The Unionists have made it clear that they will oppose fiercely any change in the status of Northern Ireland. This means that federation/confederation or any form of joint-authority will receive the veto of the majority community.

*Opposite Children
grow up fast in Belfast.
Even though the gun is
a toy, the sentiment
behind it may be real.*

Protestant suggestions

Some alternative solutions have come from the Protestants.
Full integration with Britain (with counties Antrim and
Down indistinguishable from Lancashire or Kent in terms
of local government) has been suggested, most notably by
MP Enoch Powell. Integration would arouse Irish nationalist fury, and it has no appeal to the great majority of British
politicians, whose thoughts move in the opposite direction,
toward devolvement.

Independence for Northern Ireland attracts some Protestants, including some leaders of the paramilitary Ulster
Defence Association (UDA). It is argued that the Ulster
people, Protestant and Catholic, have a distinctive northern
character and could settle down to living together if free
from either British or Irish rule. But could the leaders of
the two communities agree enough to administer Northern
Ireland harmoniously? Would Britain or the Republic accept an independent Ulster and give it the support needed
to make it work? Would the IRA accept it? All most unlikely.

Troops out?

It is believed by many that an immediate or phased British
withdrawal of troops from Northern Ireland could lead to
a bloodbath and so this alone is not a viable solution. Supporters of "Brits out" point to nearly 2,500 violent deaths
already: so why not get it over with? It is not uncommon
to overhear in Britain: "Let them fight it out!" But could
either the British or Irish governments stand by and idly
watch a civil war in Ulster that could easily be as bloody
as the recent battles in Lebanon? All the evidence points
to tens of thousands of Protestants fighting fiercely if the
status quo were threatened, as their forefathers were ready
to do in 1913.

*The "Peace Wall" in
Belfast, built to
separate the two
opposing factions.*

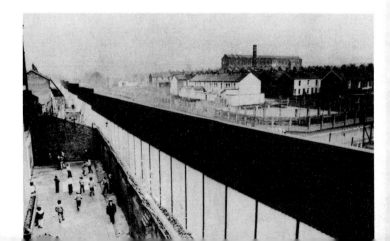

Slogans like this one are commonplace in Belfast.

A proportion of the mainly Protestant Ulster Defence Regiment (UDR) might join the Loyalist police and civilians, taking their weapons with them. Violence could even break out in Glasgow, Liverpool, and perhaps other British cities where Irish Catholics and Protestants live.

Redefining the border would not end the crisis, for large numbers of Catholics live far from the border as well as along it. Nationalists left inside Northern Ireland following the handing over of, say, south Armagh and Down to the Republic would feel more isolated and alienated than before.

Merlyn Rees, former secretary of state for Northern Ireland.

An RUC officer checks a ditch for IRA mines while another man stands guard.

However, Merlyn Rees, a former secretary of state for Northern Ireland, has suggested that letting the so-called bandit country of south Armagh join the Republic is worth discussing with Dublin. He has also recently expressed the view that Britain should consider canceling its constitutional guarantee whereby the Unionists can veto all attempts at unification.

The latest partial solution to the Irish question emerged during 1985 in the form of an agreement by the English Parliament to allow Irish representation in the government of Northern Ireland. This suggestion evoked a highly emotional response on both sides of the border.

8
The Anglo-Irish Accord

Irish Prime Minister Dr. Garret FitzGerald with Mrs. Thatcher, before the start of the Anglo-Irish summit, November 1984.

In November 1984, the British and Irish prime ministers, Margaret Thatcher and Garret FitzGerald held a summit conference in England. They announced that Anglo-Irish talks would follow, with the aim of finding an agreement in which "the identities of both the majority and minority communities in Northern Ireland [would] be recognized and respected, and reflected in the structures and processes of Northern Ireland in ways acceptable to both communities." The talks lasted a year, during which it became clear that the main problem would be whether, and to what extent, the Republic would be given a say in the running of Northern Ireland. Here again was the "Irish dimension" that had aroused Unionist anger following the Sunningdale Conference in 1973.

On November 15, 1985, Mrs. Thatcher and Dr. FitzGerald met at Hillsborough Castle, near Belfast, and signed an Anglo-Irish Accord which gave the Republic a consultative role in the running of Northern Ireland. It was the most radical political initiative since partition.

The aims of the Anglo-Irish Accord

The Accord's text said the aim of the initiative was "achieving lasting peace and stability." It recognized the rights of both communities in Northern Ireland—the Britishness of one and the Irishness of the other. Both governments agreed to respect the wishes of the majority in Northern Ireland, whether for the present status or for unification. Using the framework of the Anglo-Irish Intergovernmental Council set up in 1981, an Intergovernmental Conference would, on a regular basis, deal with: 1) political matters; 2) security and related matters; 3) legal matters, including the administration of justice; 4) the promotion of cross-border cooperation. The Irish government would be able to put forward views and proposals on these matters. "Determined efforts" would be made to resolve any differences. The conference would meet regularly and frequently at the highest level—ministerial or official. A secretariat would be set up by the two governments to service the conference. The conference would be a framework within which the two governments would work together for the accommodation of the two traditions in Northern Ireland and for peace, stability, and prosperity.

Masked IRA gunmen fire a salvo of shots over the coffin of hunger striker Raymond McCreesh, May 1983.

James Molyneaux, leader of the Official Unionist Party, announced that all fifteen Unionist MPs at Westminster would resign their seats and fight them again as a kind of mini-referendum. The unmistakable message was that if Unionist opinion was ignored there would be a policy of Unionist non-cooperation.

However, what could perhaps be an even more serious threat to the deal came from the south, where Charles Haughey, leader of the opposition Fianna Fail Party, also talked of the Accord as a "sellout," in his case of Nationalist ideals of unification. The Accord, he said, gave legitimacy to the status of Northern Ireland. Would he then repeal the agreement if he came to power? "When Fianna Fail wins the next election we will decide what to do," was his reply.

An armband of the paramilitary Third Force, with (inset) masked members of this Loyalist force on a march in Co. Down.

The IRA's response was a landmine explosion on the border which killed a policeman and seriously injured another. A Sinn Fein spokesman said the Accord showed that a united Ireland could not be achieved by constitutional means.

Once again it seems difficulties and unrest lie ahead for the people of Northern Ireland. Merlyn Rees has said of the Ulster crisis, "There is no solution, but that does not mean there is nothing to be done." Things that can be done include reconciliation and bridge building between the communities. These and other efforts that begin with individual people rather than political ideas are often described as "healing processes."

Democratic Unionist Ian Paisley with the official Unionist leader, James Molyneaux, united under the banner "Unionist Solidarity."

63

9
Healing processes

If enough people change their attitudes, the politicians will have to change theirs. In Northern Ireland changing attitudes is not easy. The difficulty was expressed cogently on a 1985 BBC television program by Mairead Corrigan. Together with Betty Williams she founded the movement of Peace People for which they won the Nobel Peace Prize in 1977. As she put it in 1985, "In order to get peace, indivi-

Mairead Corrigan (right) at the funeral of her sister who was killed in her Belfast home.

Betty Williams, co-founder, with Mairead Corrigan, of the Peace Movement.

dual people must be willing to change themselves. It's hard to grow up in Northern Ireland without being part of the bigotry, part of the tribe. Reconciliation means putting yourself in place of the other person. But very few of us in Northern Ireland are prepared to try to think as the others think ... as a Unionist, Nationalist, Protestant, Catholic, thinks ..." She summed up the nature of the problem: "We are trapped into structures in our society that make movement almost impossible."

Though individual clergy have worked courageously for reconciliation, the Churches have failed to unite because they are ideologically structured on rigid lines that stretch back to the Reformation.

Father Dermod McCarthy, whose dramatic appeal to the kidnappers of Ben Dunne, an Irish millionaire, resulted in his release, holding three bullets given to Mr. Dunne by his captors.

Segregated schooling

Because of segregated schooling combined with segregated housing, many thousands of Catholic and Protestant children grow to maturity without ever having had as an acquaintance, never mind a friend, a boy or girl who – as the saying goes – "kicks with the other foot." Lord Londonderry's 1923 Education Act had intended that Catholic and Protestant children should be schooled together, without religious instruction, but the Churches opposed this. Today Catholic and Protestant teachers are trained separately. Schools linked to specific religions are found in the rest of the United Kingdom, but there – for a variety of reasons – it does not damage the social fabric.

The few initiatives there have been in joint schooling in Northern Ireland have greatly improved understanding between young Protestants and Catholics. "They are just like us!"—the same words and tone of surprise are often heard when young people from Catholic and Protestant housing developments are brought together for the first time.

A growing sense of estrangement
Another vital healing process must be the improvement of social and economic conditions. This would reduce friction and alienation especially among the young. Northern

Small children on their way home from school are frightened as they are caught in an outbreak of fighting.

Below *A masked youth spiking a barrel of beer, during riots following the death of IRA hunger striker, Raymond McCreesh, 1981.*

Ireland has the highest unemployment rate in the United Kingdom. If there were more jobs for young people, terrorist organizations would probably find fewer recruits.

The increased sense of exclusion from their society felt by many Ulster Catholics was one area, by the mid-eighties, where both British and Irish governments saw the need for healing processes. More pointedly, the British were alarmed by one of its consequences: increased electoral support for Sinn Fein (Gaelic for ourselves), the political wing of the Provisional IRA.

Various factors fed a growing sense of estrangement from the Unionists and the British administration: most prominently what the New Ireland Forum Report called "the insensitivity of the British security policy." Internment without trial, the civilian deaths on "Bloody Sunday," the destruction by Loyalists of the attempt to run a power-sharing executive, the hunger-strike deaths, the years of failure to find a political consensus, distrust of the security forces and failure to identify with them, mass convictions of Republicans on the evidence of "supergrasses" (informers), higher rates of unemployment among Catholics—these and other complaints fed alienation, and support for Sinn Fein.

Above *A man shot dead by an army rubber bullet at a Sinn Fein rally.*

Left *August 1983: a hooded youth prepares to throw a gasoline bomb during clashes between police and Republicans.*

A Sinn Fein press conference, 1984: Danny Morrison (left), Gerry Adams MP (center) and US lawyer Richard Lawlor (right).

Politics of violence

Electoral support for Sinn Fein – who campaigned openly on a policy of "the ballot box and the armelite (rifle)" – increased from three percent of the Northern Ireland electorate in the Assembly elections of 1973, to thirteen percent in the General Election of 1983. Support for the Social Democratic and Labour Party (SDLP), the main Nationalist party, fell from twenty-two to eighteen percent in the same period.

The increase in support for Sinn Fein was one of the main reasons for setting up the New Ireland Forum in 1983. The further need to reduce Nationalist alienation can be seen in the terms of the Anglo-Irish Accord signed in November 1985. Its declared aim was greater peace and stability in Northern Ireland. John Hume, leader of the Social Democratic and Labour Party, welcomed the Accord as part of "the healing process." The immediate Unionist reaction was far from healing and it is hard to tell whether this latest potential solution will turn out to be a new dawn or a false dawn.

Since the 1960s, the problems of segregation and violence in Northern Ireland seem to have grown ever more serious.

This is partly a reflection of increased media awareness, however, as the crises of territory and identity stretch way back into Ireland's past. No one simple solution – whether violent or repressive – can erode overnight the enmity that has built up. Slow and painful as it may be, the process of healing offers some defense against further deterioration in the social fabric of the region.

A young boy takes a closer look at the security forces in action, 1981, Belfast.

Chronology

1170	Strongbow's Anglo-Norman invasion.
1171	Henry II lands in Ireland.
1172	Pope Adrian IV "grants" to Henry II the right to govern Ireland.
1541	Henry VIII takes the title "King of Ireland."
1569	Start of a series of revolts by Gaelic chiefs.
1586	Plantation of Munster.
1603	Revolts finally suppressed.
1607	"Flight of the Earls."
1608	Plantation of Ulster.
1641	The Great Rebellion begins.
1649	Oliver Cromwell lands and storms Drogheda and Wexford.
1652	The Great Rebellion finally suppressed. The Cromwellian Settlement.
1685	Accession of James II.
1688–89	Siege and relief of Londonderry.
1690	William defeats James at the Battle of the Boyne.
1783	Legislative autonomy for Ireland.
1798	Insurrection of United Irishmen.
1800	Act of Union creates United Kingdom of Great Britain and Ireland.
1867	The Fenian Rising.
1883–85	The Fenian "Dynamite War" against British cities.
1886	Gladstone's First Home Rule Bill defeated.
1893	Gladstone's Second Home Rule Bill passed by House of Commons, rejected by House of Lords.
1912	Third Home Rule Bill introduced in the Commons. 471,000 Ulster Loyalists sign anti-Home Rule Covenant.
1913	Ulster Volunteer Force (UVF) and Irish National Volunteers (INV) formed.
1914	UVF and INV both bring in rifles from Germany. World War I begins.
1916	Easter Week Rising. Leaders executed.
1919	An Irish Republic declared by Sinn Fein.
1920	Warfare between Republicans and British forces. Government of Ireland Act introduces partition.
1921	Anglo-Irish Treaty signed. Six counties become "Northern Ireland" and remain in the United Kingdom. Twenty-six counties to become the "Irish Free State."

1922–23	Civil war between pro-Treaty and anti-Treaty forces.
1937	New Irish Constitution.
1939–45	World War II. Southern Ireland neutral; Northern Ireland supports Britain.
1948	Irish Free State becomes a Republic and leaves the British Commonwealth.
1968	Civil rights movement founded. Demonstrators in Londonderry baton-charged by police.
1969	Rioting in Londonderry and Belfast ends with deployment of British troops.
1971	Internment without trial reintroduced.
1972	Troops kill thirteen demonstrators in Londonderry ("Bloody Sunday"). British Government suspends Northern Ireland's Parliament and introduces direct rule.
1973	Border referendum. Fifty-eight percent of the voting population vote to stay in the United Kingdom. Elections for Northern Ireland Assembly. Sunningdale Conference.
1974	Power-sharing Executive set up; brought down by strike of Protestant workers. Assembly dissolved.
1975	Northern Ireland Convention established.
1980	Thatcher/Haughey summit; Anglo-Irish Intergovernmental Council set up.
1981	Republican prisoners die on hunger strike.
1982	Northern Ireland Act; Assembly reconvened, but boycotted by Nationalists.
1983	New Ireland Forum.
1984	Forum Report published. Thatcher/Fitzgerald summit.
1985	Anglo-Irish Accord signed by Thatcher/Fitzgerald. Unionist opposition to Accord.
1986	Unionists at Westminster resign and refight their fifteen seats. Loyalists demonstrate against the Accord and clash with police.

Glossary

Anglo-Irish Accord Signed by the governments of the United Kingdom and the Republic of Ireland on November 15, 1985, giving the Republic a consultative role in the running of Northern Ireland.

Anglo-Irish Treaty Signed on December 6, 1921, whereby twenty-six counties of Ireland became the Irish Free State and the remaining six northeastern counties became part of the United Kingdom of Great Britain and Northern Ireland, with a Parliament in Belfast.

Devolution Transfer of business from Parliament to bodies appointed by it.

Direct rule The taking over by the British government, in March 1972, of control over law and order in Ulster. The Northern Ireland Parliament was suspended.

Fenian A member of the Irish Republican Brotherhood, founded 1858, whose goal was to free Ireland from English rule, by force if necessary.

Franchise Special privilege, especially the right to vote.

Gerrymandering Unfair manipulation of constituency boundaries.

Home Rule A semi-independent Irish Parliament in Dublin. A campaign for Home Rule was fought in the late nineteenth and early twentieth centuries.

Internment The policy, under the Special Powers Act 1922, of arresting and locking up terrorist suspects without trial.

Irish Free State On the partitioning of Ireland in 1921, the Irish Free State was the name given to the twenty-six counties that became a separate country, though within the British Commonwealth.

Irish Republican Army (IRA) The paramilitary force who fought for the Republic proclaimed in the 1916 Rising, first against the British security forces, and then against pro-Treaty Irishmen. They later turned their attentions to attempting to force the British out of Northern Ireland. In 1969, the force split into the official IRA, who had given up violence, and the provisional IRA ("the provos"), who began a terrorist campaign.

Irish Republican Brotherhood The Fenians. A secret society founded in 1858 with the aim of gaining independence for Ireland, by force if necessary.

Irish Volunteers A paramilitary force formed in Dublin in 1913 with the aim of fighting, if necessary, for Home Rule. The force split in 1914. Those willing to support the War called themselves National Volunteers.

Nationalists Supporters of an independent Ireland.

Northern Ireland The six counties of Antrim, Down, Armagh, Londonderry, Tyrone, and Fermanagh.

Orange Order Formed in 1795 to protect Protestant interests, and named after William of Orange. The Order is closely linked with Unionist politics and politicians.

Paramilitary organization An organization composed of civilians but run on military lines, like a secret army.

Partition The division of Ireland into two parts.

Pluralistic A society that tolerates and encourages within it more than one culture.

Sectarian Devoted to a particular religious denomination, especially in a nonconformist church.

Sinn Fein Gaelic for "ourselves." An Irish political party founded and led by Arthur Griffith in 1905. Eamon de Valera became leader in 1917, but left it in 1926 and founded the Fianna Fail Party. Sinn Fein has since been the political wing of the IRA.

Ulster The historic province has nine counties. Three of them in the Republic, the remaining six form Northern Ireland. However, "Ulster" is now widely used, especially by Unionists, to refer to Northern Ireland.

Ulster Defence Association (UDA) A legal paramilitary organization, formed in 1972 to protect Protestant areas.

Ulster Defence Regiment Civilian part-time soldiers recruited in Northern Ireland to support the British Army.

Ulster Volunteers A Protestant, Loyalist paramilitary force formed in January 1913 to oppose, and fight if necessary, Home Rule. Today the Ulster Volunteer Force and the Ulster Freedom Fighters are illegal.

Unionists Supporters of the union with Great Britain.

Unionist Party Began in 1905 as the Ulster Unionist Council. Became the Unionist Party in 1921 and held power in Northern Ireland for fifty years.

Index

Picture acknowledgments

The publishers would like to thank the following for providing pictures: Associated Press Ltd 10, 12, 31, 44, 47, 51, 55, 57, 69; Rex Features Ltd *Cover*; Topham Picture Library *frontispiece*, 8, 21, 23, 24, 27, 28, 30, 32, 33, 34, 35, 36, 38, 42, 46, 48, 49, 50, 52, 53, 54, 56, 58, 59, 60, 61, 62, 63, 64, 65, 66, 67, 68, 70, 71; all other pictures were provided by the Wayland Picture Library.